CORPORATE AMERICA

Johnson & Johnson

Blaine Wiseman

LIGHTBOX
openlightbox.com

LIGHTBOX

Go to
www.openlightbox.com
and enter this book's
unique code.

ACCESS CODE

LBW63653

Lightbox is an all-inclusive digital solution for the teaching and learning of curriculum topics in an original, groundbreaking way. Lightbox is based on National Curriculum Standards.

STANDARD FEATURES OF LIGHTBOX

AUDIO High-quality narration using text-to-speech system

ACTIVITIES Printable PDFs that can be emailed and graded

SLIDESHOWS Pictorial overviews of key concepts

VIDEOS Embedded high-definition video clips

WEBLINKS Curated links to external, child-safe resources

TRANSPARENCIES Step-by-step layering of maps, diagrams, charts, and timelines

INTERACTIVE MAPS Interactive maps and aerial satellite imagery

QUIZZES Ten multiple choice questions that are automatically graded and emailed for teacher assessment

KEY WORDS Matching key concepts to their definitions

Contents

Introduction

From its beginning as a small **start-up** in the late 19th century, Johnson & Johnson has grown into one of the world's largest corporations. Its long history, global reach, and corporate influence have allowed the company to become a household name throughout North America and in various parts of the world. Some of the most recognized **brands** in the fields of medication, medical supplies, and health and hygiene are Johnson & Johnson products.

The company has achieved its success through determination, innovation, and **acquisition**. Its willingness to **diversify** has made Johnson & Johnson one of the largest **holding companies** in the world. It owns and operates 275 **subsidiaries** around the world.

Johnson & Johnson created the world's **first commercial first-aid kit in 1888**.

Johnson & Johnson products are sold in **175 countries**.

Every minute, **Johnson & Johnson** makes approximately **$123,600** in sales globally.

Approximately **55 percent** of Johnson & Johnson's business is generated in markets **outside the United States**.

Johnson & Johnson's office in Madrid, Spain, houses a subsidiary company called Johnson & Johnson S.A. Founded in 1969, the company acts as a distributor for cosmetics, perfumes, and baby care products.

Johnson & Johnson

Founding Date	Became Public	Opening Price	Stock Symbol
1886	September 24, 1944	$37.50 USD	nyse: JNJ

Beginnings

A teenager during the Civil War, Robert Wood Johnson was too young to fight. He did, however, witness the widespread death and destruction caused by the war. Driven to help, Johnson decided to pursue a career in healthcare. He began with an **apprenticeship** at a pharmacy in Poughkeepsie, New York. A few years later, Johnson moved to New York City, where he worked as a salesman selling medical supplies.

While at the 1876 Centennial Exhibition in Philadelphia, Johnson attended a presentation by Joseph Lister, a renowned surgeon. Lister was promoting a new medical technique called **antiseptic** surgery. The technique used antiseptics to reduce the risk of infection. Johnson was convinced he had found the future of medicine. He wanted to help doctors improve their work conditions and treatments.

Joseph Lister was a British surgeon and scientist. He began developing his antiseptic surgery techniques while working as a surgeon at the Royal Infirmary in Glasgow, Scotland.

In 1886, Johnson joined Johnson & Johnson, a company his two brothers had started. The men opened a factory in New Brunswick, New Jersey, where they began to manufacture a line of sterile surgical products. These sutures, gauze, bandages, and absorbent cotton would become the world's first mass-produced sterile surgical materials.

From the outset, the Johnson brothers were committed to always working in the best interest of their customers. They saw it as their responsibility to make products that could help the sick recover and others live better lives. Among their early products was a book, *Modern Methods of Antiseptic Wound Treatment*, which taught doctors about the benefits of sterilization. This book helped develop the company's reputation for taking a progressive approach to healthcare.

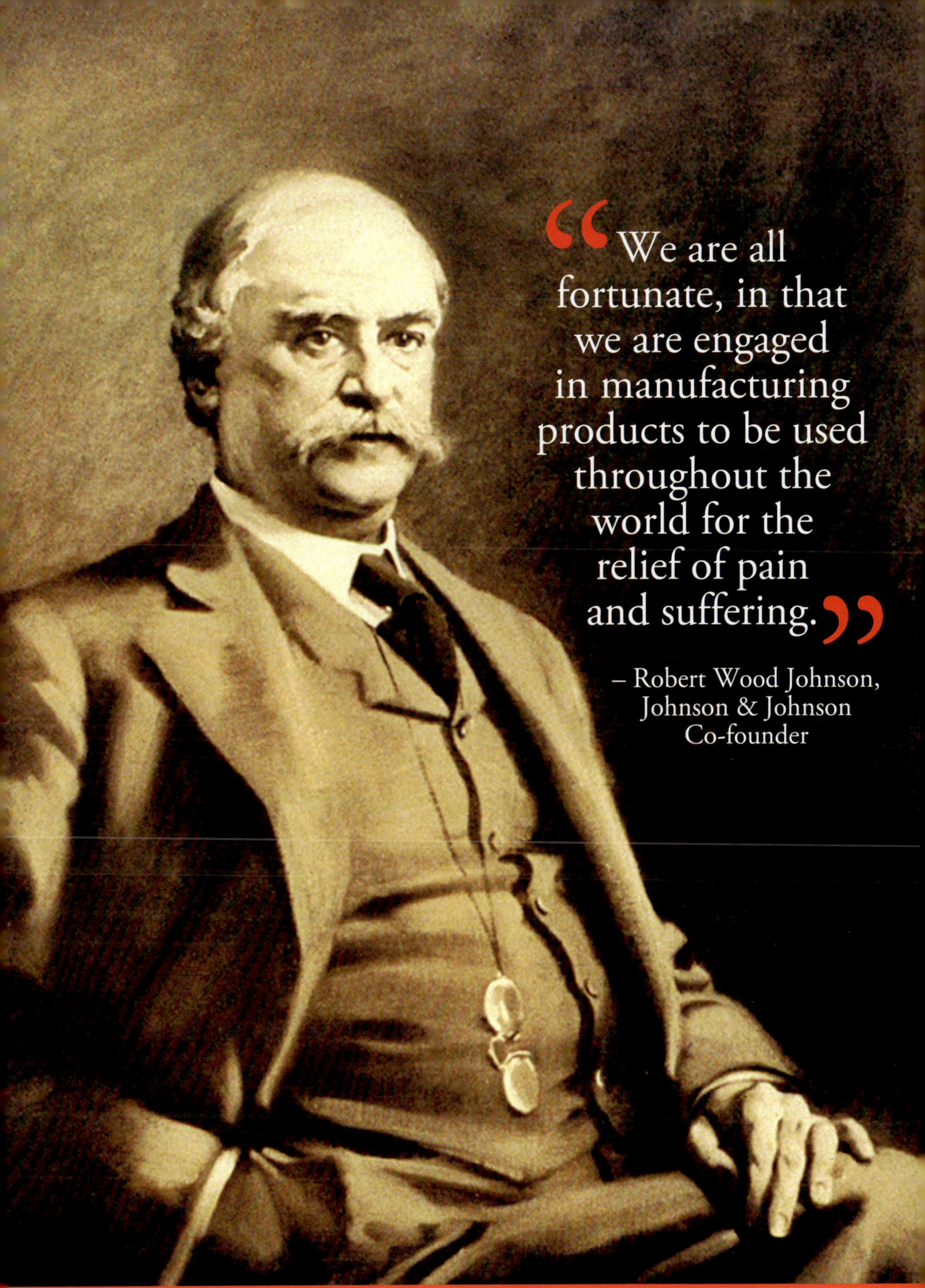

"We are all fortunate, in that we are engaged in manufacturing products to be used throughout the world for the relief of pain and suffering."

– Robert Wood Johnson, Johnson & Johnson Co-founder

Corporate Timeline

Robert Wood Johnson's foresight and innovation made a major impact on the medical world from the very beginning. His early adoption of sterilization techniques helped Johnson & Johnson grow into the corporate giant it is today. In the more than 130 years since its founding, Johnson & Johnson has achieved many more breakthroughs and milestones.

1886

Founding the Company
The Johnson brothers form their company, Johnson & Johnson, selling sterilized sutures and bandages.

1894

A Dry Comfort
Johnson & Johnson launches its baby powder product, leading to the birth of the company's baby products business.

1921

Covering Up
Band-Aid bandages are sold for the first time.

1924

Going Global
Johnson & Johnson begins operations in the United Kingdom.

1944

On Tape
In response to the U.S. Army's requests for waterproof tape, Johnson & Johnson creates the first duct tape.

1949

A New Venture
Ethicon Suture Laboratories, a Johnson & Johnson company dedicated to improving surgical techniques and products, is formed.

1954

No More Tears
Johnson's Baby Shampoo, with its "No More Tears" formula, enters the market for the first time.

1959

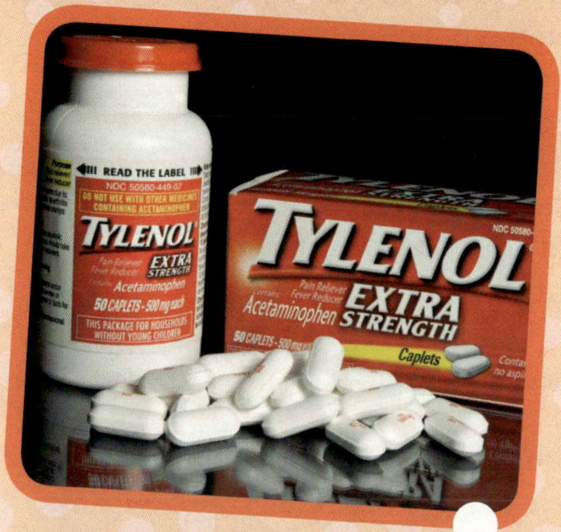

Getting Relief
Johnson & Johnson acquires McNeil Laboratories and its product, Tylenol.

1986

Adding On
Johnson & Johnson acquires LifeScan, a company that makes products to help patients cope with diabetes.

2017

A Big Purchase
Johnson & Johnson pays $30 billion to acquire Actelion, a company specializing in high blood pressure treatments.

The Company Today

Over the years, Johnson & Johnson has expanded its product line. It now has products to help people deal with many illnesses, ranging from the common cold to cancer. The wide variety of brands and products impacts the everyday lives of people of all ages and backgrounds.

Household health and beauty products are the most visible part of Johnson & Johnson's business today. Some of the most recognized Johnson & Johnson products are made for babies. Millions of people have early memories of Johnson's Baby Shampoo and Johnson's Baby Powder. Billions of cuts and scrapes have been covered up with Band-Aid bandages. Teenagers battle acne with Clean & Clear products. Tylenol and Motrin help with aches and pains. Benadryl works to stop allergic reactions.

While many of its products are used for cosmetic or minor medical issues, Johnson & Johnson still takes on bigger problems. Just as it did in the very beginning, the company leads today's medical industry with innovative surgical products and techniques. It also specializes in creating medical devices and **pharmaceutical** products that help people deal with diseases, illnesses, and injuries. Research areas include **biomedicine** and prosthetics. Products and technologies in these areas supply hospitals, clinics, and pharmacies with lifesaving drugs and equipment. Pharmaceuticals account for roughly half of the company's **revenues**.

In 2014, Johnson & Johnson's pharmaceuticals unit worked with a Danish company to develop an Ebola vaccine that could potentially save thousands of lives.

> "Across all of our businesses in every region of the world, we share a common set of beliefs ...and a common purpose: caring for the world, one person at a time. ...It is the foundation for all that we do."

– Alex Gorsky,
Johnson & Johnson
Chairman and **Chief Executive Officer** (CEO)

A World of Johnson & Johnson

Johnson & Johnson has operations in 60 countries. It is the largest and most diverse medical products company in the world. The universal need for so many Johnson & Johnson products means its **inventory** reaches almost every country on the planet.

1 **JLABS** In 2012, Johnson & Johnson opened its first JLABS facility in San Diego, California. It now operates eight JLABS across North America. These laboratories help people in the medical field develop new products.

2 **Corporate Headquarters** Johnson & Johnson's headquarters remains in New Brunswick, New Jersey, where the company started its first factory. The headquarters is housed in a 16-story high-rise office building.

3 **London Innovation Center** Located in London, England, Johnson & Johnson's London Innovation Center provides a setting for scientists to work towards advancing healthcare solutions.

4 **Janssen Pharmaceutica Headquarters** One of Johnson & Johnson's many subsidiaries, Janssen Pharmaceutica is based in Beerse, Belgium. The company focuses on finding ways to treat medical disorders such as HIV and cancer.

5 **Asia Pacific Innovation Center** Johnson & Johnson's Asia Pacific Innovation Center, in Shanghai, China, works with local and international experts to find and develop opportunities for company growth.

Branding Johnson & Johnson

Johnson & Johnson is one of the most recognized and trusted names in health and beauty. Throughout its history, the company has stood as an industry leader, helping people live longer, healthier lives. Maintaining the integrity of the brand is central to the work of Johnson & Johnson's marketing team. The company stresses the importance of quality, responsibility, and compassion in all of its work.

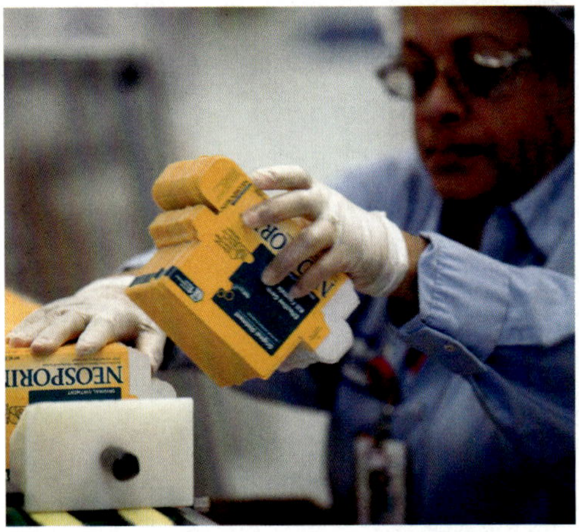

Quality From its founding, Johnson & Johnson has understood the responsibility it carries as a supplier of healthcare products. People around the world literally trust their lives to Johnson & Johnson products. Products that do not meet high standards could compromise the health of many people. The company works hard to ensure that its products undergo extensive testing. If problems occur, the company acts quickly to alert its customers and to bring the issue under control.

Culture of Caring As a healthcare provider, Johnson & Johnson believes that showing compassion and helping others is a key part of its mandate. The company demonstrates this not only through the products it creates, but through the programs it sponsors, the studies it funds, and the partnerships it forms. Every one of these projects is targeted toward helping people around the world live healthier lives. As a result of the company's efforts, more and more people are gaining access to the medicines and care they need.

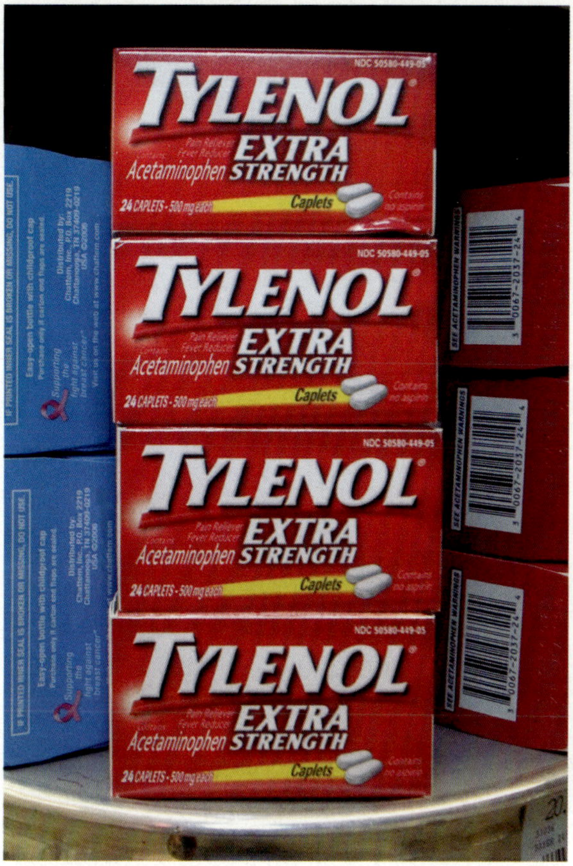

Responsibility In 1943, Robert Wood Johnson II, then chairman of Johnson & Johnson, wrote the company's **credo**. The credo emphasizes the need to be responsible to the people who rely on the company's products. These people include customers, **stockholders**, and members of the healthcare community. The company has sometimes faced challenges in this area. One instance occurred in 1982, when several people died after they took Tylenol that had been tampered with. As soon as the news reached Johnson & Johnson, the decision was made to recall every bottle of Tylenol. The recall cost the company millions of dollars, but it reassured the public that Johnson & Johnson would always do the right thing. Today, Tylenol is once again one of the country's top-selling pain medicines.

Johnson & Johnson

Company Name

The company was named Johnson & Johnson for Robert Wood Johnson's two younger brothers, Edward Mead and James Wood Johnson.

Company Logo

The Johnson & Johnson **wordmark** has been used as the company's **logo** since shortly after its founding. The logo is based on James Wood Johnson's signature.

Company Slogan

The company **slogan**, "Caring for the world, one person at a time" is integral to its brand messaging. It reinforces the company's core values in a simple, easy-to-understand manner.

The Art of Selling

Johnson & Johnson has created a variety of marketing campaigns over the course of its history. These campaigns market both individual products and the company itself. Some of the campaigns introduced a new perspective of the company. Others relied on established images that have been proven to resonate with consumers.

For All You Love Launched in 2013, this global campaign focused on bringing Johnson & Johnson's products together under one brand image. Advertising for the campaign was designed to sell Johnson & Johnson itself, rather than individual products. The ads focused on how people care for those they love, and Johnson & Johnson's place within those relationships. Each advertisement in the campaign ended with the words "for all you love." This phrase was meant to capture the emotion that people feel for those in their care.

Having a Baby Changes Everything In 2002, Johnson & Johnson began running ads that focused on the changes parents experience when a baby is born. Called "Having a Baby Changes Everything," the ads compared how a person perceives life before and after he or she becomes a parent. The emphasis was on how one little person becomes the center of a parent's universe. The creation of these ads was meant to show that Johnson & Johnson understands what people go through when they have a baby and that the company is there to provide support through trusted products and services.

See the Real Me In 2014, Johnson & Johnson launched a video series on YouTube. Entitled #SeeTheRealMe, the series promoted the company's Clean & Clear skin care line. However, instead of openly selling products, the series focused on interviews with young women, ranging from ordinary teenagers to celebrities. In these interviews, the women discussed the lives they lead and the challenges they face. The campaign had more than 30 million views within its first year. People who watched the videos also learned about the Clean & Clear product line.

Johnson & Johnson's
U.S. marketing budget in 2015 alone was
$1.12 billion.

Johnson's Baby products earned the company more than **$2 billion** in 2016.

More than
400 people
work in **Johnson & Johnson's**
global marketing department.

Competitors

With such a wide range of products and business interests, Johnson & Johnson also has a wide variety of competitors. These competitors range from multinational drug manufacturers to independent cosmetic companies. Pharmaceutical giants such as Pfizer, medical device companies such as Medtronic, and health and beauty **conglomerates** such as L'Oréal Group are the major competitors in each field.

Pfizer **STOCK SYMBOL** nyse: PFE

Based in New York City, New York, Pfizer is one of the world's largest pharmaceutical companies. Some of Pfizer's top-selling products are medications that help lower **cholesterol**, manage pain, and cope with arthritis. Pfizer is a leader in over-the-counter treatments, offering products such as Advil to compete directly with Johnson & Johnson's Tylenol.

Medtronic **STOCK SYMBOL** nyse: MDT

Founded in Minneapolis, Minnesota, in 1949, Medtronic is the industry leader in the field of medical technology. The company's products are dedicated to surgery and recovery from medical procedures, injuries, and illnesses. Medtronic strives to make operations cleaner, less invasive, and more effective. It focuses much of its work on the development of **cardiovascular**, diabetes, and spinal health products.

L'ORÉAL **STOCK SYMBOL** epa: OR

L'Oréal Group was founded in Paris, France, more than 100 years ago. Today, it is the world's largest cosmetics and beauty company. Much of its portfolio comes into direct competition with Johnson & Johnson's consumer products division. L'Oréal product lines such as Biotherm, Garnier, and Lancôme compete directly with Johnson & Johnson's Neutrogena, Lubriderm, Aveeno, and Clean & Clear products.

Comparison Chart

Businesses keep records to track their **assets**, **liabilities**, **profits**, and losses. Companies use this data to guide expansion and cost-cutting decisions. Investors use the information to help them decide where to invest their money. They will also refer to a company's **market capitalization** to gauge public confidence in the business.

2016 Figures

Innovation and Technology

JLABS

Johnson & Johnson has committed to advancing healthcare by helping scientists become **entrepreneurs**. To assist in this process, the company operates a series of research facilities across North America. JLABS gives scientists the tools, funding, and expertise they need to make medical breakthroughs. Through JLABS partnerships, small companies developing new products in medical care use Johnson & Johnson resources to bring their ideas to fruition. These companies can share information and resources across the JLABS network to advance the science behind what they do.

SIRTURO

For decades, tuberculosis (TB), an infectious lung disease, was successfully treated with drugs called isoniazid and rifampin, along with several others. Over time, however, one strain of TB became resistant to these drugs. A new drug was needed to stop the spread. In 2012, Johnson & Johnson's subsidiary, Janssen Pharmaceutica, received government approval for its new drug, SIRTURO. It was the first new anti-TB drug to be approved since 1998, and the science behind its development is seen as a major step forward in the treatment of TB. This breakthrough could lead to millions of lives saved.

Skin-Flex Band-Aids

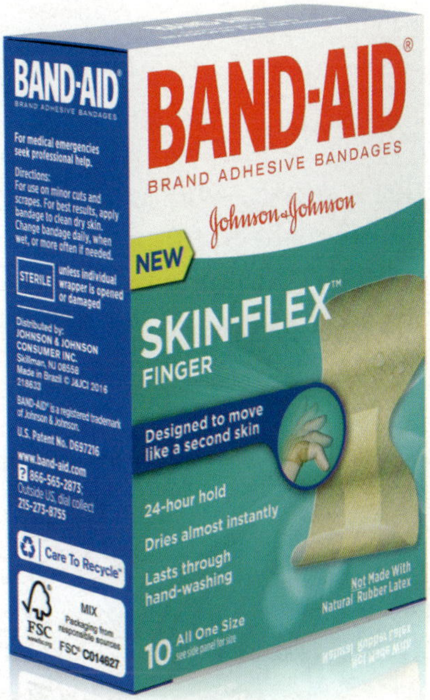

While many Johnson & Johnson products save lives, others simply help people lead better lives. One thing that can evolve even more quickly than diseases and treatments is technology. Smartphones and tablets are a major part of people's lives today. A bandage on a finger can make touch screens on these devices more difficult to use. In response to this problem, Johnson & Johnson developed a line of Band-Aids using touch screen-friendly material. Skin-Flex Band-Aids use modern technology to solve a modern inconvenience.

The Allergy App

Many people experience seasonal allergies. Most occur in the spring and fall when pollen is in the air. Allergy medications do much to relieve allergy symptoms. However, Johnson & Johnson discovered that people were often taking their medications even when pollen levels were low and there was little risk of an allergy flare-up. To provide people with updates on pollen levels, the company developed an **app** called AllergyCast. All a person has to do is enter their zip code, and the app provides the pollen level for the area, along with an allergy risk score. This helps allergy sufferers to use their medication more effectively.

Giving Back

Johnson & Johnson is committed to the communities it serves, whether it is a small area or the world as a whole. This commitment is realized not only through medical breakthroughs and treatments, but also through charitable works and community involvement. Each year, Johnson & Johnson and its employees spend millions of dollars and thousands of hours helping to make a difference in their communities and around the world.

Volunteer Leave Since helping people is such a major part of Johnson & Johnson's business, the company encourages its employees to volunteer for causes that are important to them. The company's Extended Volunteer Leave program grants employees two weeks off, with one week paid, in order to spend more time volunteering with **non-profit organizations**. With more time to volunteer, employees have the option of traveling to other locations to lend a helping hand. They can also stay in their own community and help others in a more dedicated fashion than their work hours would typically allow.

Bridge to Employment Started in 1992, Johnson & Johnson's Bridge to Employment (BTE) program helps students in the United States and around the world prepare for careers in the health sector. The program begins with high school sophomore students and continues through to graduation. During the three-year program, students are given opportunities to grow and succeed. Students can job shadow at Johnson & Johnson and its partner companies, as well as attend workshops at universities. In its 25-year history, between 30 and 40 percent of BTE participants have gone on to pursue careers in the health and science fields.

Health for Humanity 2020 Health for Humanity 2020 is a Johnson & Johnson initiative designed to foster positive change around the world by the year 2020. The program focuses on three main areas—people, places, and practices. Helping people focuses on developing medical solutions for those in need. To help places where it operates, Johnson & Johnson is striving to use fewer natural resources. To improve its practices, the company is working with its suppliers to ensure they are using healthy, sustainable practices. The company is also encouraging employees to live better lives through healthy eating and exercise habits.

For every $1 a Johnson & Johnson employee donates **to a charity**, the company **donates $2.00**.

100% of **Bridge to Employment participants** have gone on to graduate from high school.

As part of the **Health for Humanity program**, **Johnson & Johnson** plans to obtain **35% of its electricity** from **clean or renewable resources** by 2020.

Into the Future

Even though Johnson & Johnson has grown into one of the world's most successful corporations, this growth has not come without challenges. Still, the company has been able to survive and even thrive during difficult situations. The ability to adapt will remain a strength as the company maneuvers itself through a rapidly changing marketplace.

In the healthcare industry, the area currently experiencing some of the greatest change is pharmaceuticals. From evolving illnesses and diseases to new ways of treating them, it takes a great deal of resources and work to stay on top. Some of Johnson & Johnson's top-selling pharmaceutical products are in danger of being overtaken by newer products from competitors. The company is committed to staying ahead of the competition. In 2017, it announced its plans to introduce 10 new drugs by 2021.

Johnson & Johnson's development of JLABS and innovation centers is meant to encourage new solutions to the world's health problems. The company plans to open more of these facilities in the future. It also plans to continue its tradition of acquiring other companies. In doing so, it hopes to expand its healthcare capabilities even further. For instance, the company's recent purchase of Actelion gives Johnson & Johnson access to Actelion's medications. Not only will this help Johnson & Johnson financially, it will also allow for information to be shared between the two companies. This has the potential to bring even more improvements to global health care.

In 2017, Johnson & Johnson announced that it will open a new JLABS in New York City. Scheduled to open in 2018, the JLABS will be located in the New York Genome Center, a facility dedicated to medical research.

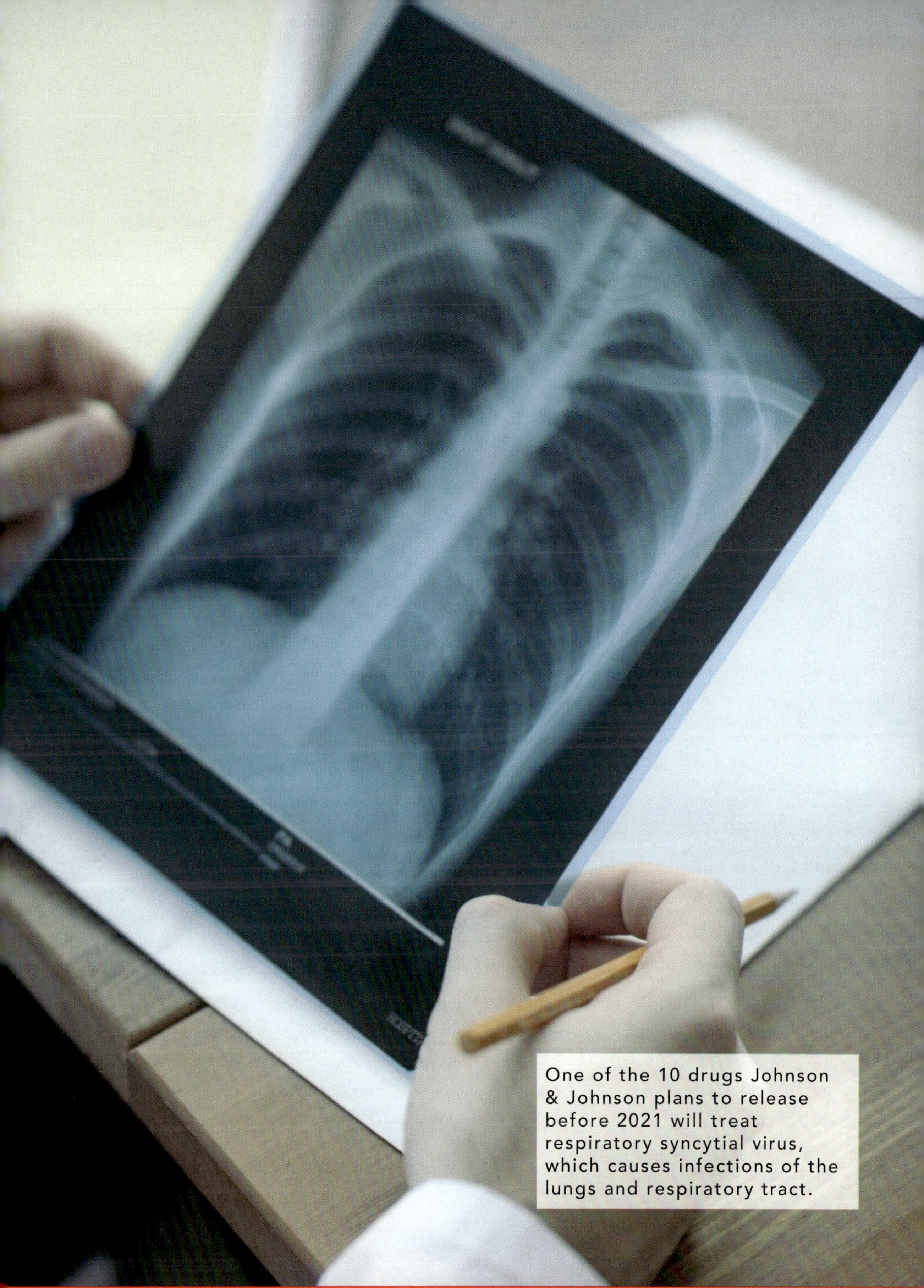

One of the 10 drugs Johnson & Johnson plans to release before 2021 will treat respiratory syncytial virus, which causes infections of the lungs and respiratory tract.

Careers at Johnson & Johnson

With more than 125,000 employees around the world, and hundreds of subsidiary companies, there is no shortage of work at Johnson & Johnson. From researching and designing new products to planning their marketing campaigns, Johnson & Johnson employees perform thousands of different tasks. Each employee plays an important role in the growth and well-being of the corporation.

CEO

$26.8 million per year

The CEO is usually the highest position in a company. The person who holds this position is responsible for creating and executing the company's long-term goals. A CEO is in charge of all aspects of the business. He or she decides whether a company will undergo expansions. The CEO oversees all departments and branches within the company, managing staff and delegating tasks. Generally, CEOs hold a high-level business or management degree.

Scientist

$60,275–$127,830 per year

Johnson & Johnson scientists work to find solutions and breakthroughs in the medical field. Many different areas of expertise are represented at Johnson & Johnson. These range from chemistry and biology to more specialized areas such as **molecular pharmacology**. Using their extensive knowledge, scientists perform tests and experiments, analyze data, and work with other researchers to develop new products and processes.

Software Engineer

$35,000–$72,000 per year

Software engineers build, implement, and maintain the systems that make the company run. They solve problems relating to existing and speculative products within the company. Designing and running tests, building prototypes, and weighing the benefits versus the drawbacks of new technologies are major parts of a software engineer's job.

Statistician

$103,000–$130,000 per year

Statisticians analyze the data and statistics of Johnson & Johnson, its markets, and its competitors. They plan research and tests. Statisticians also prepare reports and create models and simulations to demonstrate the values of various statistics. Upon completion, they then work with senior managers to apply the results to the company's future plans.

Activity

Johnson & Johnson is constantly seeking new ways to advance the medical industry. The company's research facilities focus their attention on finding new treatments and equipment to treat illnesses and other medical conditions. Some of these are for everyday disorders, such as allergies and acne, while others help people who are suffering from rare diseases.

Imagine that Johnson & Johnson has developed a new product to treat either a common health ailment or a serious disease. What would you like that product to be? Plan a marketing campaign for this new product. Use the following questions to develop your campaign.

1. Who do you want to buy your product?
2. What are the key selling points of your product?
3. What types of marketing materials will be needed to reach your target market?
4. What types of language and designs will you use to attract your buyers?
5. Where will you place your advertising?

Quiz

1 Whose presentation did Robert Wood Johnson attend in Philadelphia in 1876?

2 Who wrote Johnson & Johnson's credo?

3 How many subsidiary companies does Johnson & Johnson own?

4 Which Johnson brother's signature was used to create the company's logo?

5 What is the name of the company that Johnson & Johnson bought in 2017?

6 Which company is Johnson & Johnson's biggest competitor in the beauty industry?

7 Which part of the business accounts for about half of the company's revenues?

8 Which Johnson & Johnson program helps students prepare for work in the healthcare field?

9 Which Johnson & Johnson subsidiary developed the drug SIRTURO?

10 Who is the current CEO of Johnson & Johnson?

Answers

1. Joseph Lister's **2.** Robert Wood Johnson II **3.** 275 **4.** James Wood Johnson **5.** Actelion **6.** L'Oréal Group **7.** Pharmaceuticals **8.** Bridge to Employment **9.** Janssen Pharmaceutica **10.** Alex Gorsky

Key Words

acquisition: the purchase of another company

antiseptic: something that prevents the growth and spread of germs

app: a software program used on desktop computers and mobile devices

apprenticeship: working for someone to learn a trade

assets: valuable properties owned by a company or person

biomedicine: a branch of medicine that uses natural processes to treat illnesses

brands: products that identify a company

cardiovascular: having to do with the heart and blood vessels

chairman: a person designated to preside over a meeting

chief executive officer (CEO): the highest-ranking person in a company

cholesterol: a fat-like substance that occurs naturally in the body's cells

conglomerates: companies made up of several divisions

credo: a statement of beliefs

diversify: to enlarge or vary a company's range of products

entrepreneurs: people who organize and operate their own business

holding companies: firms that own controlling interest in other companies

inventory: a complete list of merchandise on hand

liabilities: a company's debts and costs

logo: a symbol or design used to identify a specific company

market capitalization: the value of a company's outstanding shares

molecular pharmacology: the study of how chemicals affect biological processes at the cellular level

non-profit organizations: groups that conduct business for the benefit of the general public without a profit motive

pharmaceutical: medicinal drug

profits: the money left over after business costs are subtracted from sales

revenues: the amount of money a company receives for goods or services sold over a particular amount of time

slogan: a distinctive phrase used to identify a specific company or product

start-up: a fledgling business

stockholders: people who own shares, or stock, in a company

subsidiaries: companies owned by another company

wordmark: the official style in which an organization's name is written

Index

LIGHTBOX

SUPPLEMENTARY RESOURCES

Click on the plus icon found in the bottom left corner of each spread to open additional teacher resources.

- Download and print the book's quizzes and activities
- Access curriculum correlations
- Explore additional web applications that enhance the Lightbox experience

LIGHTBOX DIGITAL TITLES
Packed full of integrated media

VIDEOS

INTERACTIVE MAPS

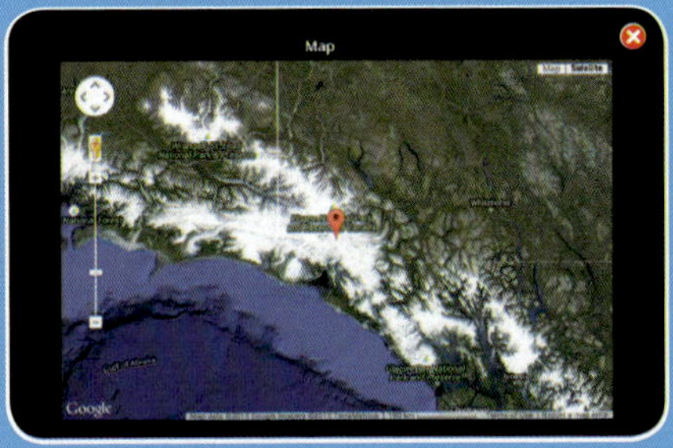

WEBLINKS

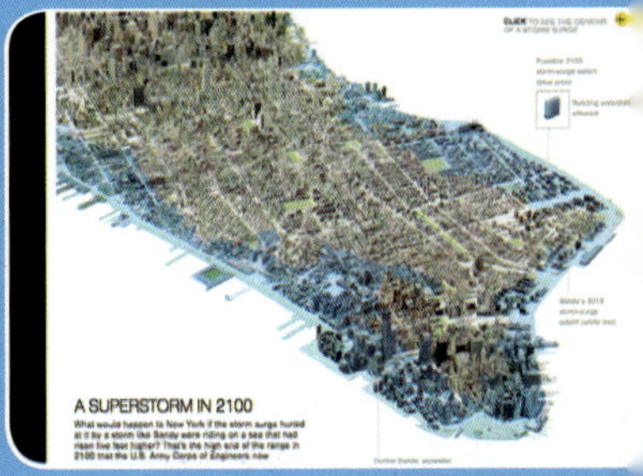

SLIDESHOWS

QUIZZES

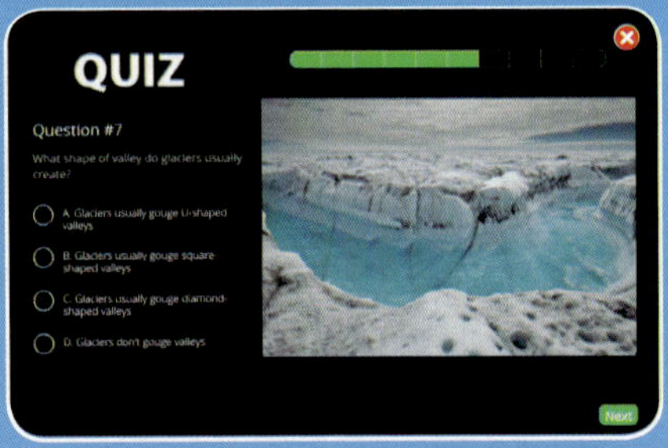

OPTIMIZED FOR

- ✓ TABLETS
- ✓ WHITEBOARDS
- ✓ COMPUTERS
- ✓ AND MUCH MORE!

Published by Smartbook Media Inc.
350 5th Avenue, 59th Floor New York, NY 10118
Website: www.openlightbox.com

Editor: Heather Kissock
Designer: Nick Newton

Library of Congress Cataloging-in-Publication Data
Names: Wiseman, Blaine, author.
Title: Johnson & Johnson / Blaine Wiseman.
Description: New York, NY : Smartbook Media Inc., [2019] | Series: Corporate America | Includes index.
Identifiers: LCCN 2017048290 (print) | LCCN 2017049835 (ebook) | ISBN 9781510534957 (Muli-User Ebook) | ISBN 9781510534940 (hardcover : alk.paper)
Subjects: LCSH: Johnson & Johnson--Juvenile literature. | Pharmaceutical industry--United States--Juvenile literature.
Classification: LCC HD9666.9.J6 (ebook) | LCC HD9666.9.J6 W57 2019 (print) |DDC 338.7/6161510973--dc23
LC record available at https://lccn.loc.gov/2017048290

Printed in Brainerd, Minnesota, United States
1 2 3 4 5 6 7 8 9 0 21 20 19 18 17

122017
151217

Photo Credits
Every reasonable effort has been made to trace ownership and to obtain permission to reprint copyright material. The publisher would be pleased to have any errors or omissions brought to its attention so that they may be corrected in subsequent printings. The publisher acknowledges Alamy, Getty Images, Newscom, iStock, and Shutterstock as its primary image suppliers for this title.